No levels available 3/17

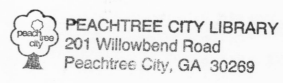

# CHRISTOPHER COLUMBUS
## Discovery of the Americas

# CHRISTOPHER COLUMBUS
## Discovery of the Americas

## Clint Twist

RSVP

**RAINTREE**
**STECK-VAUGHN**
PUBLISHERS

The Steck-Vaughn Company

*Austin, Texas*

FLINT RIVER REGIONAL LIBRARY

**Series Editor:** Su Swallow
**Editors:** Nicola Barber, Shirley Shalit
**Designer:** Neil Sayer
**Production:** Peter Thompson
**Consultant:** Bruce M. Taylor, University of Dayton

Maps and Illustrations: Brian Watson, Linden Artists

**Library of Congress Cataloging-in-Publication Data**
Twist, Clint.
    Christopher Columbus: the discovery of the Americas / Clint Twist.
       p.  cm. — (Beyond the horizon)
    Includes index.
    Summary: Introduces the background, voyages, discoveries, and historical significance of Christopher Columbus.
    ISBN 0-8114-7253-1
    1. Columbus, Christopher — Juvenile literature. 2. Explorers — America — Biography — Juvenile literature. 3. Explorers — Spain — Biography — Juvenile literature. 4. America — Discovery and exploration — Spanish — Juvenile literature. [1. Columbus, Christopher. 2. Explorers. 3. America — Discovery and exploration — Spanish.] I. Title. II. Series.
E111.T89 1994
970.01'5—dc20
                                                93-19017
                                              CIP  AC

Printed in Hong Kong
Bound in the United States

1 2 3 4 5 6 7 8 9 0 LB 99 98 97 96 95 94 93

# Acknowledgments

For permission to reproduce copyright material the author and publishers gratefully acknowledge the following:

**Cover** (top left, top middle) Michael Holford, (top right) Werner Forman Archive, (middle left) Ronald Sheridan, Ancient Art & Architecture Collection, (bottom left) National Maritime Museum, Greenwich/Werner Forman Archive, (bottom right) Robert Harding Picture Library
**Title page** (Replica of the Niña) Jonathon Nance
**page 4** (top) Mary Evans Picure Library, (bottom) Robert Harding Picture Library **page 5** (top) Archiv für Kunst und Geschichte, Berlin/Image Select, (bottom) Robert Harding Picture Library **page 6** Robert Harding Picture Library **page 7** (left) Michael J. Howell, Robert Harding Picture Library, (right) Michael Holford **page 8** Ronald Sheridan, Ancient Art & Architecture Collection **page 9** (top) Ronald Sheridan, Ancient Art & Architecture Collection, (bottom) Michael Holford **page 10** Anne Rippy, The Image Bank **page 11** Michael David/ Ronald Sheridan, Ancient Art & Architecture Collection **page 14** Ronald Sheridan, Ancient Art & Architecture Collection, Archiv für Kunst und Geschichte, Berlin/Image Select **page 15** Michael Holford **page 16** Ronald Sheridan, Ancient Art & Architecture Collection **page 17** Robert Harding Picture Library **page 18** Jeff Foott Productions, Bruce Coleman Ltd **page 19** (top) Mary Evans Picture Library/Explorer, (bottom) Michael Holford **page 20** Guido Alberto Rossi, The Image Bank **page 21** Juergen Schmitt, The Image Bank **page 23** Robert Harding Picture Library **page 24** Ronald Sheridan, Ancient Art & Architecture Collection **page 25** (top)Mary Evans Picture Library, (bottom) Archiv für Kunst und Geschichte, Berlin/Image Select **page 26** (top) British Museum /Robert Harding Picture Library, (bottom) Michael Holford **page 27** (top) British Museum /Robert Harding Picture Library, (bottom left) Kerstin Rodgers, The Hutchison Library, (bottom right) Ann Ronan Picture Library **page 28** (top and bottom) Robert Harding Picture Library **page 29** (top) Ronald Sheridan, Ancient Art & Architecture, (bottom) Archiv für Kunst und Geschichte, Berlin/ Image Select **page 30** Archiv für Kunst und Geschichte, Berlin/ Image Select **page 31** (top, bottom) Sotheby's **page 32** (top) Stuart Franklin **page 33** (top) The Mansell Collection (bottom) Michael Holford **page 34** (top) Michael Holford, (middle) Anthropology Museum, Veracruz University, Jalana/ Werner Forman Archive, (bottom) J.G. Fuller, The Hutchison Library **page 35** Ronald Sheridan, Ancient Art & Architecture Collection **page 36** (top) Robert Francis, Robert Harding Picture Library **page 37** (top) Walter Rawlings, Robert Harding Picture Library, (bottom) Eric Lawrie, The Hutchison Library **page 38** Robert Harding Picture Library **page 39** Werner Forman Archive **page 40** Robert Harding Picture Library **page 41** (top) Luis Castenada, The Image Bank **page 42** (top) Archiv für Kunst und Geschichte, Berlin/Image Select, (bottom) The Hulton-Deutsch Collection **page 43** Leonard Freed, Magnum Photos

# Contents

# Introduction

One of the many portraits of Christopher Columbus, none of which, as far as we know, were painted from life.

Although America had no silks or spices, it did have precious metals. Below: a gold figure from Mexico.

## "In fourteen hundred and ninety-two Columbus sailed the ocean blue."

These traditional lines of school day verse remind us that the year 1492 is one of the great signposts in the history of the human race. For it was on October 12, 1492, that Christopher Columbus reached land after his first voyage westward across the Atlantic Ocean. He had sailed west to try to find a sea route to the rich lands of the East. Instead, he reached a land unknown to Europeans: America.

It is important to understand exactly why 1492 is so significant. We are not really remembering the exploits of a single Italian sea captain, no matter how skillful and daring he may have been. Columbus did not "discover" America. There were probably already between 60 to 100 million native inhabitants living on both continents, and they had explored most of it. What Columbus did was to introduce America to Europe, and Europe to America. The result of this introduction was the creation of what Europeans called the "New World" – a land of dreams and opportunity, and also a land of nightmares and destruction.

### Eastern horizons

It was only a matter of time before Europe discovered America. By the end of the 15th century, European society had grown restless. New ideas about art, science, and religion, and new inventions such as printing, had combined to produce an atmosphere of change. Europeans were looking beyond their limited horizons, particularly toward the East. The lands of India, China, and Japan were very wealthy in gold, silks, and spices. However, traveling to the East meant making the same long, overland journey as Marco Polo. The person who discovered a way to sail to and from the East would undoubtedly become very rich.

Columbus's belief that the world was round convinced him that he could reach the East by sailing west. But he was mistaken. Unexpectedly, Columbus found America blocking his route.

### A bad beginning

History is not always pleasant. Sometimes when people read about events in history they feel angry or ashamed. The discovery of America by Christopher Columbus is a story of European achievement. Yet there are parts of his story, and parts of the history of America after 1492, that must make most Americans of European background feel at least slightly ashamed.

Slaves in a 19th-century ship. Slaves being transported to America were crammed tightly together below decks.

Christopher Columbus was a tough, greedy man. He was a brave leader, but a careless administrator. Many of those who followed him to America were of similar character. Through ignorance and greed they destroyed the Aztec and Inca civilizations, and caused the death of about eight out of every ten Native Americans. When there were no longer enough natives to work in the mines and fields, the Europeans began importing black slaves from Africa. Millions of black people were shipped to America to work in chains. The effects of this slave trade are still being felt today.

However, the judgment of history must not be too harsh. Columbus, and the Spanish conquerors who followed him to America, lived in times very different from our own. By today's standards, they were appallingly ignorant. If we think that they behaved badly, it is only because we have since learned better. Christopher Columbus and his crew were, after all, just a small group of human explorers in tiny ships, floating on the vastness of the Atlantic Ocean.

## Horizons

After reading this book, you may want to find out more about some aspect of Columbus's discovery. Or you may become interested in a particular place or topic. At the end of some of the chapters, you will find **Horizon** boxes. These boxes list the names of people, places, ideas, and objects that are not mentioned in the book, but which are nevertheless part of the story of Christopher Columbus and America. By looking them up in the indexes of other reference books, you will discover more about Columbus and his time.

## The Vikings and Vinland

Columbus was not the first European to "discover" America. The Vikings had sailed here about 500 years earlier. Originally from Norway, the Vikings sailed first to Iceland and then to Greenland, where they set up colonies. Approximately A.D. 1000, Eric the Red sailed his longship westward until he sighted land (the coast of Canada). The Vikings named their discovery Vinland, and established a small settlement. But the Vinland settlement did not last very long, probably because of attacks by hostile Native Americans. Later, the Vikings abandoned their Greenland colony as well, and Europe soon forgot all about the lands across the Atlantic.

A replica of a Viking ship.

# The Historical Background

### Columbus – a life at sea

Christopher Columbus was born in either 1451 or 1452 in the Italian seaport of Genoa. His family were all weavers, but for some reason young Christopher did not follow the family trade. Instead, when he was about 14 years old, he went to sea.

The city of Genoa already had a long tradition of seafaring. At one time, Genoa had competed fiercely with the city of Venice for a share of the valuable trade in silks and spices across the eastern Mediterranean. The Venetians had won the trade war, and the Genoese had turned their attention to the west. In 1291, Genoese sailors became the first Christians to sail through the Strait of Gibraltar out into the Atlantic Ocean.

As a young trainee, Columbus sailed around the Mediterranean coast. Later, he signed up for longer voyages into the Atlantic. By the time he was 26 years old he had sailed as far south as the island of Madeira, and as far north as Iceland.

The port of Genoa today. The old city – where Columbus lived – is in the foreground.

### Atlantic exploration

In 1477, Columbus married and settled in Lisbon, the capital of Portugal. At this time, the Portuguese were Europe's most

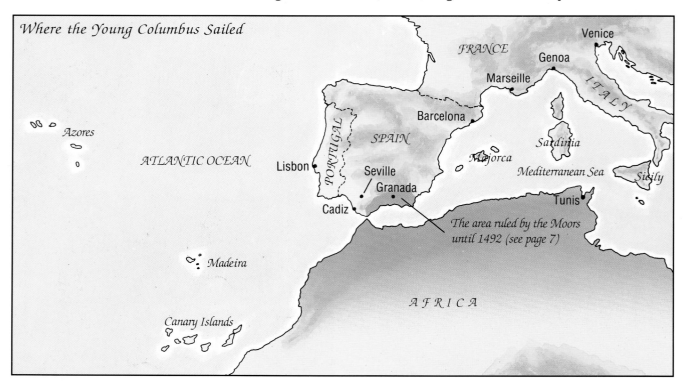

*Where the Young Columbus Sailed*

FRANCE

Venice

Genoa

Marseille

Barcelona

ATLANTIC OCEAN

Azores

PORTUGAL

SPAIN

Sardinia

Majorca

*Mediterranean Sea*

Sicily

Lisbon

Seville

Granada

Tunis

Cadiz

*The area ruled by the Moors until 1492 (see page 7)*

Madeira

AFRICA

Canary Islands

ITALY

adventurous sailors. Under the leadership of Prince Henry "the Navigator" (1398-1460) Portugal established a principle that was to dominate European thinking for the next 300 years – exploration by sea can bring great wealth.

The coastal waters to the north of Portugal were already well known. But to the south of Portugal lay waters that were comparatively unknown. The triangle of ocean bounded by the Canary Islands off the West African coast, the Azores farther out in the Atlantic, and the Portuguese coast is often known as the Atlantic Mediterranean because it was first explored around 1350 by Genoese and Majorcan sailors. However, by the 1420s Portuguese sailors had taken the lead in the exploration of this area and had accurately mapped all its various islands.

Venturing farther south along the coast of Africa, the Portuguese discovered that they could obtain two valuable commodities – gold and slaves. The lure of easy money led to more exploration, and by the time of Prince Henry's death, Portuguese ships had sailed as far south as Sierra Leone.

## The position of Spain

Spain was larger and more powerful than Portugal. It, too, had ports on its Atlantic coast – Cadiz and Seville (reached by river). But as yet Spain had no real interest in the Atlantic. During most of the 1400s, Spain's attention was concentrated elsewhere. One immediate problem was that part of the country was still under Islamic control. A sizeable region of southern Spain around the city of Granada was controlled by Moors, a Moslem people who

The Alhambra, a fortress built by the Moorish rulers of Granada in Spain. Inside, the Alhambra is beautifully decorated (right: a courtyard).

had invaded Spain from North Africa in the 8th century. However, Spain's Mediterranean coastline had been free from Islamic influence for several centuries. Spanish ships, operating from ports such as Barcelona, had made the country a powerful force and, by the 1460s, the Spanish king ruled Sardinia, Sicily, and the southern half of Italy.

Although the old Islamic Empire of the Arabs was in decline, it had been replaced by the Turkish Ottoman Empire based in Istanbul (formerly the Christian city of Constantinople). At around the same time that the Spanish king acquired southern Italy, the Turkish sultan was completing his conquest of Bulgaria, Greece, and Yugoslavia. The blue waters of the Mediterranean Sea were besieged by these rival powers. The only way for other Christian kingdoms to increase their power and wealth was to turn their attention to the gray waters of the Atlantic Ocean.

## A time of transformation

In 1477, the year that Columbus settled in Lisbon, Europe stood poised at the very end of the Middle Ages. Life had changed little during the previous 300 years. There was one Church, the Roman Catholic Church, headed by the pope. Printing had only just been invented and books were rare. During the next 100 years Europe was completely transformed by a series of discoveries, inventions, and new ideas. Some of this change was the result of Columbus's own achievement. His voyage to America marked the beginning of a great Age of Discovery, during which European ships would explore every corner of the world's seas and oceans. European art and religion also changed dramatically during this time.

## The Renaissance and the Reformation

European art had been devastated by the collapse of the Roman Empire in the A.D. 400s, and it took nearly a thousand years to recover. Most of the paintings and sculpture produced in Europe before 1400 look crude when compared with the art of ancient Greece and Rome. Around 1450, artists working in northern Italy started to study ancient Greek and Roman art. As a result, artists such as Leonardo da Vinci (1452-1519) began to produce more realistic paintings and sculpture. This development is known as the Renaissance (rebirth) of European art.

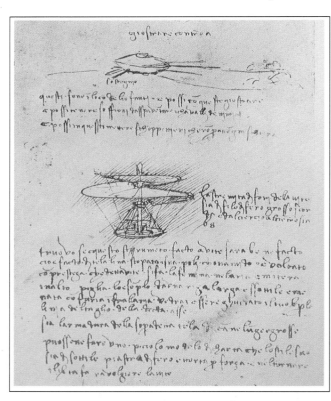

A page from Leonardo da Vinci's notebook. He was an inventor as well as an artist. These are his designs for a fighting machine and a flying machine.

The study of ancient art led to a new interest in ancient science and philosophy, and some scholars began to question the teachings of the Catholic Church. These questions developed into a philosophy known as humanism, which encouraged scientific

Martin Luther preaching Protestantism.

discovery. Humanism spread rapidly around the universities of Europe. Many students came into conflict with the Church over matters of education, because at this time all students also had to be priests. By the 1520s, protesters against the Catholic Church had established their own, Protestant Church. This split is known as the Reformation.

The leading figure of the Reformation was the German priest and scholar, Martin Luther (1483-1546). Luther demanded reforms of the Catholic Church, and when these were refused in 1521, he declared an independent Church. He was supported by the leaders of some German states, and opposed by others. Religious wars broke out, but the Protestant states of Germany managed to survive.

The Catholic Church tried to suppress the attacks of humanism and Protestantism by force. Catholic reaction was strongest in Spain, which although far from the center of disputes among Christians, was at war with Islamic Moors for control of the country. In 1481 Spain reintroduced the Inquisition (see box) which had originally been used by the Church to search out and punish heretics — people who questioned the accepted version of Christianity taught by the Church. Under the Grand Inquisitor Torquemada, the Spanish Inquisition also persecuted humanists, Jews, and Islamic converts to Christianity.

# The Inquisition

The Inquisition was a Church court that was originally intended to deal with heretics and witches. A heretic was a Christian believer who disagreed with or questioned the teachings of the Catholic Church.

The first Inquisition was set up in Italy during the early 1200s, and the idea soon spread to other countries. The Inquisition was rather like a religious "secret police." The Inquisitors relied on informers to bring them information about suspected heretics, and they often tortured their suspects to make them confess. The normal punishment for witches and heretics was to be burned at the stake. Around 1380 the Inquisition began to decline. It was revived in Spain in order to punish those who were not loyal to the Catholic Church. Later, the Spanish Church turned its attention abroad. In 1534 a Spanish nobleman, Ignatius Loyola (1491-1556), founded the Society of Jesus. Teachers and missionaries from this society, often known as the Jesuit Order, carried their stern brand of Catholicism to all parts of the world.

A Spanish religious painting showing the Inquisition burning books. Usually their activities were not quite so peaceful.

## A man of his time

In 1477 all these transformations lay in the future, and in some ways the Renaissance and Reformation have no part in Columbus's story. Columbus never met Leonardo da Vinci, and he died before Luther began teaching. However, these developments do help our understanding of Columbus, because he was very much a man of his time. The same society that shaped the Renaissance and Reformation also shaped Christopher Columbus. Like Leonardo, Columbus was adventurous and ambitious; and, like Luther, he was convinced that he was right.

For several years, Columbus continued to sail under the flag of Portugal, venturing as far south as the Cape Verde islands and beyond, around the bulge of Africa. Meanwhile, he dreamed of sailing to the unknown East in search of riches.

## Eastern promise

Although silks and gemstones were more showy, spices were the real treasure of the Far East – people wanted to be able to flavor their food. So anyone who could find an easier route to the source of spice was bound to find fame and fortune.

Columbus had become obsessed with the wealth of the Far East. The distant lands of India, China, and Japan were said to be rich in silks, spices, gemstones and, in particular, gold. Unfortunately, nobody could be certain that these countries actually existed because no European had been there within living memory. In fact, the last man to do so had been Marco Polo — nearly 200 years before.

Marco Polo had written a book about his travels, describing the wealth of the Far East in great detail. In Columbus's time Marco's book was the basis for all European knowledge about the lands to the east of the Mediterranean. Columbus had his own copy of the book, an expensive item when books were still a luxury. Wherever Marco referred to geographical position, Columbus made his own notes in the margin. He was especially interested in Japan, where the houses were supposed to be roofed in gold. Marco stated that Japan lay to the east of China.

Columbus's reasoning was simple. If the world was round, which he believed, then he could sail to Japan by heading west across the Atlantic Ocean. According to his calculations, Japan lay about 2,700 miles to the west of the Canary Islands. A long voyage, but not impossibly long. The hardest part was getting other people to believe in him.

## The search for support

Columbus could not set out to explore by himself; he could not even afford the cost of one ship, let alone the three ships that his plan required. In 1484 he put his plan to the Portuguese king, but it was turned down. The Portuguese were more interested in Africa than in some fabled lands that might lie to the west. In order to protect its interest in Africa, Portugal had made a treaty with Spain in 1479. The two countries had divided the Atlantic

Ocean so that Spain ruled the Canary Islands and Portugal was granted everything to the south. Columbus then took his plans to Spain. The Spanish rulers set up a committee to examine his ideas. For seven long years Columbus stayed at the Spanish court, trying to influence the king and queen. Twice his plan was rejected, but he did not give up. Finally, in 1492, Columbus obtained the official support of Queen Isabella of Spain.

Why was Columbus successful? He was not the only foreigner at the Spanish court with such a scheme. What did Isabella see when she heard him plead his case at the beginning of 1492? Columbus was obviously a very experienced sailor and navigator, and had sailed as far north and south as any man alive. He would be loyal to whoever employed him: earlier in his career, Columbus had happily fought a sea battle on the side of the Portuguese against his home city of Genoa. He was also ambitious and greedy. In return for discovering a sea route to Asia, Columbus demanded that he should be knighted and made an admiral. He also laid claim to ten percent of all the riches that he might bring back from the voyage.

Something about Christopher Columbus made Queen Isabella believe that he would succeed.

Ferdinand and Isabella, king and queen of Spain.

## Spanish fortunes

The year 1492 would have been exceptional for Spain, even without Columbus's achievement. At the beginning of the year, Spanish armies finally reconquered the territory of Granada held by the Moors. Spain was at last united and free of Islamic occupation. Although the discoveries of Christopher Columbus were disappointing at first, in the end they led to huge financial gains for this new, unified Spanish state.

## Horizons

You could find out about these people who all lived at around the same time as Christopher Columbus: Mohammed II (Ottoman Turkish sultan); Lorenzo "the Magnificent" Medici (Italian banker, businessman, and politician); Erasmus (Dutch humanist philosopher); Thomas More (English politician and philosopher); Niccolò Machiavelli (Italian politician); Michelangelo (Italian artist); Sandro Botticelli (Italian artist); Albrecht Dürer (German artist).

## The Unification of Spain

In the 8th century, most of Spain and Portugal had been invaded and occupied by Islamic people, called Moors, from North Africa. As Spain was reconquered by Christian forces two powerful and independent kingdoms were created — Aragon in the north, and Castile in the center. In 1479, these kingdoms were united by the marriage of Isabella of Castile to Ferdinand of Aragon, and the country of Spain was created.

Early in 1492, Spanish troops finally conquered the last region held by the Moors — Granada in the south of the country. The unification of Spain was at last complete.

# Modes of Transportation

## Tiny ships on the ocean

One of the most astonishing aspects of Columbus's achievement was the small size of his ships. On his first voyage of discovery, the largest ship measured only about 79 feet in length.

European sea trade was well established by this time, although it was largely confined to coastal waters. Large ships regularly transported goods between the Baltic Sea and Mediterranean countries, carrying up to 1,000 tons of cargo at a time. There were two sorts of ship engaged in this long-distance trade: cogs and carracks. The largest cogs and carracks were up to 198 feet long, and more than 66 feet wide. On the rough waters of the Atlantic Ocean, large ships were more stable than smaller ones.

Columbus had spent much of his time at sea aboard cogs and carracks. However, he chose to use much smaller craft when he went exploring.

## The discovery fleet

When he set sail in 1492, Columbus's fleet consisted of just three ships. Between them they could carry barely 200 tons of supplies and cargo. The largest was the *Santa Maria* (90 tons), next the *Pinta* (60 tons), and smallest was the *Niña* (45 tons) which was less than 66 feet long.

The flagship of the fleet was the *Santa Maria*. Unfortunately, nobody is quite sure exactly what sort of a ship it was. The *Santa Maria* was certainly not a cog or a carrack. Columbus describes the ship as a *nao*, which is not very helpful because the word simply means "ship." We do know that the *Santa Maria* was less than 83 feet long, with a single deck along the whole of its length. At the bow there was a second raised deck, and at the stern there were two additional decks. Three masts carried square sails, and the main mast had a lookout platform at the top.

The *Pinta* and the *Niña* were both Portuguese-style caravels. The caravel was originally built as a fishing boat to be used in the choppy waters of the Atlantic. By Columbus's time, caravels had developed into small all-purpose craft that had proved their worth during the Portuguese exploration of the African coast. A caravel had three or four masts that usually carried triangular lateen sails. Rigged in this way, the caravel was known as a *caravela latina*.

At first, the *Niña* had two masts with triangular lateen sails. However, when Columbus's fleet reached the Canary Islands on the first voyage, he mounted two additional masts on the caravel and fitted square sails. In doing so, he converted the *Niña* from a *caravela latina* to a *caravela redonda*, which was to prove much more suited to the winds of the Atlantic Ocean.

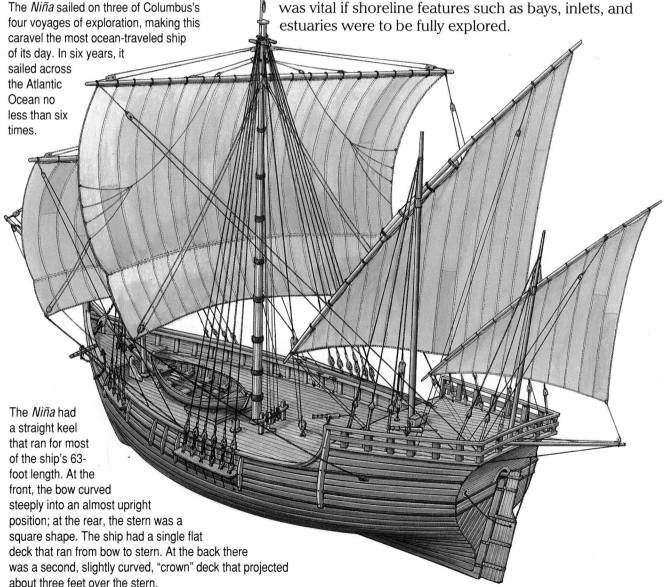

The *Niña* had ten of these cannons, known as *bombardas,* and was equipped with 80 lead balls and nearly 110 pounds of gunpowder.

Columbus's favorite of his three ships was the *Niña*, the smallest. From an explorer's point of view, such a small ship had a number of advantages. Caravels had a shallow draft because they were originally designed for coastal fishing, and they needed only about seven feet of water in which to float. This shallow draft meant that caravels could sail very close to unknown shores. A small ship also meant a small crew. The *Niña* probably sailed with no more than five officers and 16 sailors. A small crew was easier to keep friendly and cheerful on a long voyage. This was important as an unhappy crew might be liable to mutiny. A small crew also meant that the ship needed to carry less food and drink. Everything that the crew would need on the voyage, including drinking water, had to be packed on board before leaving land.

One other advantage of the caravel was that the ship was small enough to be towed by a single rowboat. This was vital if shoreline features such as bays, inlets, and estuaries were to be fully explored.

The *Niña* sailed on three of Columbus's four voyages of exploration, making this caravel the most ocean-traveled ship of its day. In six years, it sailed across the Atlantic Ocean no less than six times.

The *Niña* had a straight keel that ran for most of the ship's 63-foot length. At the front, the bow curved steeply into an almost upright position; at the rear, the stern was a square shape. The ship had a single flat deck that ran from bow to stern. At the back there was a second, slightly curved, "crown" deck that projected about three feet over the stern.

## A varied cargo

Columbus carried with him official letters of greeting from the rulers of Spain to the emperor of Japan. But he was also prepared for an unfriendly welcome. All of his ships were armed with small cannons.

Since their introduction during the previous century, use of gunpowder weapons had become widespread throughout Europe. Columbus's ships were too small to carry wheeled cannons on deck. Instead, cannons were fitted on swivel mountings along the rail at the highest parts of the ship. Other weapons carried by members of the crew included spears, swords, and crossbows.

Despite their small size, caravels could carry quite a load. For Columbus's third voyage, the *Niña* was crammed with more than 50 people (21 crew and 36 colonists), and nearly 50 tons of cargo. Life on board was extremely cramped, and at night everyone had to sleep on the open deck. Below deck every available space was filled with cargo, mostly supplies for the colonists. Food was cooked on deck in a large copper cauldron over an open fire that was set in a sandbox for safety. The main items of cargo carried were: 18 tons of wheat; 17 tons of wine stored in huge barrels; 7 tons of sea biscuits (very hard and dry); 2 tons of flour; 1 ton of salt pork; 1 ton of cheese. Additional items included olive oil, sardines, raisins, and garlic.

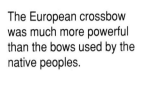

The European crossbow was much more powerful than the bows used by the native peoples.

## Round or Flat?

The most important item carried by the first transatlantic fleet was the captain's firm belief that the world was round. This was not a new idea, and it was the only logical explanation for the movement of the sun, moon, and stars. Ancient Greek astronomers had even calculated the circumference of a round earth. However, this ancient learning had been lost after the collapse of the Roman Empire, and was not rediscovered until the beginning of the Renaissance.

By Columbus's time the idea that the world was round was shared by many educated men. Columbus had been in contact with the Renaissance mathematician, Paulo Toscanelli, who had calculated that Japan must lie about 2,700 miles west of Spain. Unfortunately there was a mistake in Toscanelli's calculations. It was pure coincidence that America happened to lie where he thought Japan was. However, most of the sailors on Columbus's ships were uneducated and superstitious men who still believed that the world was flat. Most of them probably feared that Columbus was planning to sail off the map, and literally off the edge of the world.

One of the first globes, from 1492.

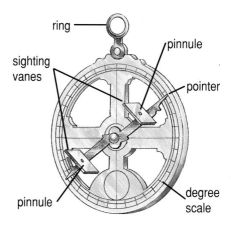

The astrolabe was used to measure the angle between the horizon and the sun, called the altitude. A navigator held the astrolabe up by the ring, turning the sighting vanes until the sun was lined up through both holes, or pinnules. The pointer gave the altitude in degrees.

A 16th-century hourglass.

## Steering and navigating

Like nearly all European ships of this time, the *Niña* was steered by a single hinged rudder that hung from the stern. But it had not always been so. Until around 1300, European ships had been steered by a pair of large oars, one on each side of the stern. This arrangement was clumsy and made steering difficult. The stern-hung rudder was a great improvement because it meant the ship could be steered by only one sailor.

The rudder was operated by a lever mounted at the stern between the two decks. In front of this steering position was fixed the "mariners' needle," the compass. The compass, a Chinese invention, had become widespread by Columbus's day. It enabled a 15th-century navigator to steer a fairly accurate course.

Fixing a ship's position at sea was much more difficult than steering a course. Latitude, the position north or south, could be approximately measured by a variety of fairly simple instruments. The cross-staff was a device for measuring the angle between the horizon and a particular star. The backstaff was used to measure the angle between the horizon and the sun. The astrolabe was, in Columbus's day, a new instrument copied from the Islamic Empire, which had in turn inherited it from the Greeks and Romans. Columbus's crew distrusted the astrolabe, and plotted to throw their captain overboard when they saw him using one.

Fixing a ship's longitude, the position east or west, was even more uncertain. The best method was to work out the distance sailed by multiplying the ship's speed by the length of time it had been sailing. However, with the winds and currents constantly shifting, measuring the ship's real speed was very difficult. Furthermore, the only way of telling the time was by using an hourglass, in which sand ran from one end to the other. Columbus was so unsure about the distances that he was traveling that he had to lie to his crew to keep their spirits up.

## Columbus's plan

Columbus's plan was essentially very simple and required only one change of course. From the small Spanish port of Palos de la Frontera, his ships would sail southwest to the Canary Islands. This was a familiar route for Columbus. After replenishing their supplies, the fleet would then sail directly westward until they reached the coast of Japan. Throughout this westward leg of the voyage, Columbus would have to take care not to stray south into waters controlled by the Portuguese under the 1479 treaty (see page 10).

# The Voyages of Christopher Columbus

A 16th-century picture showing Columbus leaving Spain, watched by Queen Isabella and King Ferdinand.

## The first voyage (1492-93)

On August 3, 1492, Christopher Columbus sailed out of the harbor at Palos de la Frontera, and set a southerly course for the Canary Islands. The *Santa Maria* and the *Niña* made good time, and covered the 600 miles in nine days. The *Pinta* was less fortunate when, after just four days at sea, its rudder broke off. Columbus left the crippled caravel to make its own way to the Canary Islands. The *Niña's* lateen sails were also a problem. Although these were perfectly suited to sailing in the Mediterranean Sea, they were less efficient in the Atlantic than the square sails carried by the other two ships.

Columbus spent longer in the Canary Islands than he had expected. Rerigging the masts and sails on the *Niña*, and replacing the *Pinta's* broken rudder, took a long time. Finally, Columbus sailed west on the morning of September 6, 1492.

## Across the Atlantic Ocean

Tradition has it that Columbus now sailed due west, for day after day. As the days turned into weeks the crew became more and more unhappy with the voyage. In order to keep their spirits up, Columbus promised a reward of 10,000 gold coins to the first sailor to sight land.

After a month at sea, Columbus altered course and turned southwest, making straight for where he believed Japan should be. The sight of birds and pieces of floating wood now convinced

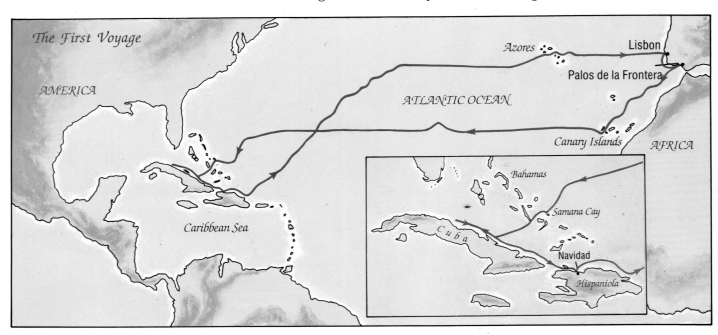

The First Voyage

AMERICA

ATLANTIC OCEAN

Azores

Lisbon

Palos de la Frontera

Canary Islands

AFRICA

Caribbean Sea

Bahamas

Cuba

Samana Cay

Navidad

Hispaniola

First sight of the New World. It is not known exactly where Columbus landed, but it was probably somewhere very like this.

most of the crew that land was indeed close by. Three days later, he altered course again, this time to the west, and sent the *Pinta* ahead of the other two ships. Finally, at 2 A.M. on October 12, 1492, the lookout on the *Pinta* saw moonlight gleaming on distant cliffs. After 37 days at sea, they had found land. Later that morning the fleet anchored in a sheltered bay, and a rowboat took a party ashore to the land that Columbus believed was Japan.

## Around the islands

After wading ashore, Columbus immediately claimed the land as the territory of the king and queen of Spain, and named it San Salvador (Holy Savior). His next task was to find out exactly where in the islands of "Japan" he had landed. Historians today face a similar problem. It is now thought that the present-day island called San Salvador is not the island where Columbus landed. Columbus's log does not give enough information for historians to be certain about exactly where in the Caribbean Islands he did land. Various locations have been suggested, the most likely ones being near Samana Cay in the Bahamas.

The native inhabitants of the island were friendly, but not very helpful. Using sign language, they indicated that their gold ornaments came from the next island. For two weeks, Columbus's ships sailed from island to island, always getting the same answer to their questions – "the next island." When they reached Cuba, Columbus was convinced that they had arrived in China. He sent a party of sailors inland to search for the city of Zaitun, which had been described in detail by Marco Polo. However, the party came back and reported nothing but a small group of thatched huts. Disappointed, Columbus split his fleet, and sent the *Pinta* off separately, while he sailed south with the *Santa Maria* and the *Niña*. On December 23, he arrived at a large island which he named La Isla Española (the Spanish Island), and which is today called Hispaniola.

## The first settlement

Columbus's ships were greeted by a large group of natives, many of whom happily handed over pieces of gold. Then news arrived that seemed to suggest that the emperor of Japan lived just a short distance along the coast. Columbus immediately set sail, but a day later disaster struck. At around midnight on Christmas Eve the *Santa Maria* sailed onto a coral reef and became firmly stuck. As water poured through the damaged hull, Columbus abandoned ship and his crew scrambled ashore.

They spent an anxious Christmas in a native village, while Columbus decided what to do. The main problem was that the *Niña* could not possibly carry all of the *Santa Maria*'s crew as well as its own. Eventually, Columbus decided to leave a party of settlers behind. The *Santa Maria* was taken apart, and the ship's timbers were used to build a fort, which Columbus named Navidad (Nativity) because it was Christmas. Altogether, some 39 sailors stayed in Navidad, including carpenters, a tailor, and a doctor. Columbus left instructions for them to collect as much gold as possible. He also left behind some of the *Santa Maria*'s cannons to be used to defend Navidad if necessary.

A manatee, an aquatic mammal sometimes mistaken by early sailors for a mermaid!

## Homeward bound

The *Niña* now sailed on alone along the coast of Hispaniola. At one point, Columbus sighted three mermaids, who "were not as beautiful as artists paint them." In fact, Columbus had seen three manatees, large mammals that inhabit shallow, tropical waters. Farther on, a party of sailors from the *Niña* came across hostile natives for the first time. The sailors had gone ashore to pick fruit when they were attacked by about 50 natives armed with clubs and bows and arrows. They managed to chase the natives away before anyone was killed.

The *Niña* now met up with the *Pinta* and the two caravels set a northeasterly course for home. At first they made good progress, but after about three weeks they ran into a violent storm, and the two ships were separated. Sailing on alone in the *Niña*, Columbus arrived at the Azores, where the Portuguese governor put half his crew in prison on suspicion of being smugglers. Columbus managed to free his sailors, and quickly set sail straight into another huge storm. The *Niña* was badly damaged, and only just stayed afloat long enough to reach the Portuguese capital, Lisbon, on March 4, 1493.

Painted tiles showing Columbus presenting the evidence of his discoveries to the Spanish court.

## A triumphal return

Columbus quickly repaired the *Niña*, and a week later he sailed for Spain. On March 15, the *Niña* sailed back into the harbor at Palos de la Frontera to be welcomed by the cheering townsfolk. By a strange coincidence, the *Pinta* arrived just a few hours later, having missed the Azores and made much slower progress. Columbus's triumph was now complete. Two of his three ships had completed the voyage, and none of them had been lost in the open sea.

Columbus carried with him proof that he had been somewhere that was previously unknown to Europeans. He brought back exotic plants and animals, such as pineapples and parrots, that had never been seen in Europe before, as well as gold worked into strange masks and ornaments. He also brought back a handful of native captives from the Caribbean Islands as living proof of his achievement.

Summoned to the royal court, Columbus made a triumphal journey across Spain, accompanied by some of his crew and the native captives. All along his route, the crowds turned out to cheer Spain's new admiral, and to stare in amazement at his strange trophies. Even at the hour of his greatest triumph, Columbus remained a very greedy man. He insisted on claiming the 10,000 gold coins reward for himself, and the disappointed sailor who had in fact first sighted land ran away and joined a pirate ship.

Columbus's reward may well have contained coins like this one, which bears the portraits of Ferdinand and Isabella.

The island of Guadeloupe, skirted by coral reefs.

## The second voyage (1493-96)

Columbus's second voyage was much grander than the first. He commanded a fleet of 17 ships, carrying somewhere between 1,000 and 1,500 people. Some of these were settlers, eager to start a new life in what Europeans called the "New World." Others were fortune hunters who planned to make themselves rich by collecting gold from the natives. Surprisingly, the Spanish king and queen seem to have been more interested in farming than in gold. They saw the future of their new territories as agricultural settlements which would produce food to feed Spain's growing population. They were also most concerned that the native inhabitants of the New World should be converted to Christianity as quickly as possible. For this reason, a group of missionary priests and monks traveled with the fleet.

The ships assembled at the Spanish port of Cadiz, and the fleet sailed on September 25, 1493. Once again, Columbus sailed first to the Canary Islands to restock with fresh food and water. On leaving the Canary Islands, he set a southwest course, hoping this time to arrive at the mainland of what he still thought was Asia.

## The fate of Navidad

The three-week voyage passed without incident, and on November 3 the lookout on the lead ship sighted land. Columbus named this island Dominica, but did not bother to stop. The next day, the fleet found and named the island of Guadeloupe, and

later the island of Puerto Rico. However, Columbus was not really interested in discovering more islands – he was obsessed with the idea of reaching the mainland. He was also eager to revisit Navidad in the hope that the men he had left behind would have collected a huge amount of gold.

When the fleet did reach Navidad, they found only the charred remains of the fort and a few European bodies. There were no survivors. The massacre of Navidad must have seemed like a disaster to the settlers waiting anxiously on board ship. By talking with the natives, Columbus managed to discover the truth.

The sailors left behind at Navidad had become too greedy. They had demanded that the natives deliver more gold than they could obtain. They had also begun kidnapping natives and making them work as slaves. Although the natives were friendly, the behavior of the Europeans had provoked them to violence. One night, the tribes had assembled and attacked Navidad, burning the buildings and killing all the European settlers.

## The quest continues

Columbus had to take decisive action. He led the fleet slowly around the coast of Hispaniola until he found a suitable site for a new settlement. Columbus named this new town Isabella, in honor of the Spanish queen. Clearing land and laying the foundations of Isabella took several months. After this work was completed, Columbus led an expedition inland on another

The island of Puerto Rico. Away from the coastline, the islands found by Columbus were covered by dense rain forest.

fruitless search for the source of the natives' gold. Returning to Isabella, he found the work behind schedule and he handed out harsh punishments to some of the lazier settlers. At the end of April 1494, he left Isabella under the command of his younger brother and sailed off with three ships to find the elusive mainland.

A month later he discovered Jamaica, but this turned out to be yet another island. Deeply frustrated, Columbus now became convinced that Cuba (discovered on his first voyage) was in fact the mainland of Asia. While suffering from a tropical fever he made everyone on board the ships swear, on pain of having their tongues torn out, that Cuba was definitely part of the Asian mainland. The fleet finally returned to Isabella at the end of September.

## Another failure

For the next year and a half, Columbus struggled to make Isabella work, but he had made a bad choice of site. Insects and disease made life very difficult, and food was always in short supply. The local natives had also become a serious threat to the settlement's survival. Only a very few, who had become Christians, continued to see the Europeans as friends. Columbus did not help the situation when he sent 500 native slaves back to Spain as a present to the king and queen. During the winter of 1495-96, the natives started a violent rebellion which was only quelled with difficulty. In March 1496 Columbus returned to Spain, leaving orders that Isabella be abandoned and a new settlement built during his absence.

## The third voyage (1498-1500)

Although the loss of Navidad and the failure of Isabella counted against him, Columbus was still in favor at the Spanish court. Even so, it took him two years to arrange his next expedition. This time Columbus had planned a different approach. From the Canary Islands he sailed southward to the Cape Verde Islands. Then he sailed southwest for ten days, before turning west. This time he felt certain of finding the mainland of Asia.

In fact, the first land that the fleet encountered was the island of Trinidad. A few days later they reached the coast of Venezuela, and Columbus became the first European to set foot

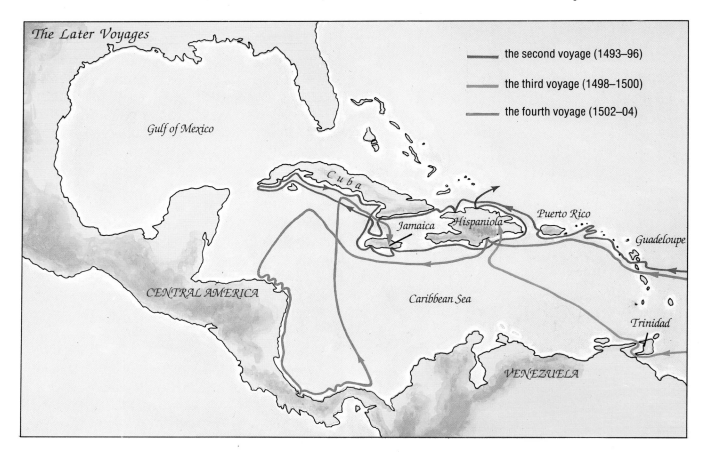

The Later Voyages

— the second voyage (1493–96)

— the third voyage (1498–1500)

— the fourth voyage (1502–04)

Gulf of Mexico

Cuba

CENTRAL AMERICA

Jamaica

Hispaniola

Puerto Rico

Guadeloupe

Caribbean Sea

Trinidad

VENEZUELA

A Spanish-style cathedral in Santo Domingo.

on the mainland of South America. Certain that this was indeed Southeast Asia, he then sailed north to Hispaniola. On arriving at the new town of Santo Domingo, which still stands today, he found many of the settlers rebelling against his authority. Columbus quickly rounded up the ringleaders, and sent to Spain for a senior official to investigate the rebellion.

On his arrival, the official announced that he was taking charge, and that Columbus was to return to Spain. The king and queen had decided that, while Columbus was a great explorer, he was a bad governor. As a gesture, Columbus insisted on sailing back to Spain in chains, as though he were a common prisoner. On seeing Columbus in chains Queen Isabella took pity on him, and allowed him to go into retirement.

## The fourth voyage (1502-04)

Although Columbus probably realized that the land he had discovered was not Asia he was still determined to find a route to India and China. After much pleading, he managed to persuade the Spanish government to allow him to make one last attempt. This time he had only three small ships. They sailed on April 3, 1502, and crossed the Atlantic without difficulty, but among the islands of the Caribbean they ran into a hurricane. Through skillful seamanship, Columbus survived the hurricane and soon arrived at the mainland of Central America. For months they sailed down the coastline, looking vainly for a sea passage to India. Storms forced Columbus to abandon his search, but he had left it too late. On the way back to Hispaniola he was shipwrecked on the coast of Jamaica. For a whole year he and his crew lived a miserable existence, surrounded by hostile natives. They built a fortress for themselves using wood from the damaged ships. For food, they traded glass beads and hawkbells for cassava bread, fish, and corn.

Eventually, two sailors made a dugout canoe and managed to reach Hispaniola, a journey of over 102 miles. A ship was sent to rescue Columbus, who was by this time very ill. His final return to Spain was far from triumphant, a far cry from the return from his first voyage (see page 19). Columbus died two years later on May 20, 1506, and was given only a poor funeral.

## Horizons

You could find out about some other people associated with the discovery of America: Francisco de Bobadilla (who replaced Columbus as governor of Hispaniola); Juan Ponce de León (who discovered Florida); Alonso Morales (a Spanish mapmaker); Bartolomé de Las Casas (the "Apostle of the Indians," one of the few Europeans who tried to help Native Americans); Hernández de Córdoba (who explored the coast of the Yucatán Peninsula).

# A New World Discovered

The discovery of the New World was one of the most important events in European (and world) history. During the last 500 years, many artists have painted the event. Usually, as above, Columbus is shown as a hero. In fact, he was a greedy and insensitive leader, who showed little consideration for the peoples and cultures that he "discovered."

### A New World

Although the Vikings had crossed the Atlantic some 500 years before he did (see page 5), Christopher Columbus undoubtedly "discovered" America from a European point of view. Before Columbus sailed, Europe was essentially a Mediterranean civilization. The boundaries of the known world were scarcely wider than those of the ancient Roman Empire. Despite the advances of the Renaissance, Europe was still very inward-looking. With a single daring voyage, Christopher Columbus opened up a whole new world of exploration and overseas trade for Europe. In 1490, the longest sea voyages were no more than 720 miles. Columbus sailed more than three times that distance before sighting land. By 1500, voyages of 2,400 miles had become quite common.

## The age of exploration

In an age without newspapers or television, news of Columbus's voyages spread remarkably quickly. Within seven years of his return to Spain, two other European nations had staked a claim to different parts of the New World.

In 1497 another Genoese navigator, Giovanni Caboto (better known as John Cabot), sailed west from England in search of India. Cabot's expedition had the support of the English king, Henry VII. Like Columbus, Cabot had been appointed governor of any lands that he might discover. John Cabot sailed from the port of Bristol on board a ship named the *Mathew*. Five weeks later, he sighted land which he mistakenly identified as the Mongol Empire described by Marco Polo. The *Mathew* sailed along some 360 miles of coastline, but found little of interest except large numbers of codfish. The region Cabot discovered is now known as Newfoundland and Labrador in eastern Canada. The following year, Cabot made a second voyage with five ships, only one of which returned. Cabot himself was lost at sea. His son, Sebastian, ventured farther north and south in search of a northwesterly route to India. However, floating pack ice and rough weather made the search for this northwest passage extremely hazardous.

In 1500 the Portuguese navigator Pedro Cabral sailed south from Lisbon. After 47 days he sighted the coast of Brazil and made landfall near the present-day town of Vera Cruz. Cabral

Amerigo Vespucci.

then turned eastward to sail around Africa, following the route pioneered by another Portuguese sailor, Vasco da Gama. During the next two years, the coast of Brazil was explored farther in the name of Portugal by Amerigo Vespucci. Although Vespucci made no major new discoveries, he gave such exaggerated reports of his explorations that the whole of the New World was named after him: Amerigo's land – America.

In 1513 Vasco Balboa traveled overland from a Spanish settlement in Central America, and became the first European to gaze on the Pacific Ocean. Somewhere over the horizon, across thousands of miles of open sea, lay the distant riches of India and China. Fortunately for Spain, the riches of America lay much closer to hand.

## From exploration to conquest

The West Indies were quickly explored and mapped. The islands had good agricultural land, but they were lacking in exotic spices and gold. As a result, the Spaniards soon turned their attention to the mainland of Central America.

The native inhabitants of the mainland were not all simple tribespeople. Great civilizations had developed in America, completely independently of the rest of the world. The fact that these civilizations were not Christian was unacceptable to the

## Mapping the New World

Some 50 years before Columbus's voyage, Johannes Gutenberg had perfected the European invention of printing. As people's interest was stimulated by the new thinking of the Renaissance, there was a massive increase in the number of books and mass-produced illustrations. Maps quickly became very popular. Before 1492, the western edge of a world map was usually decorated with mermaids and sea monsters. Columbus's voyage soon changed that.

The first world map to show the New World was produced in Germany in 1507 by Martin Waldseemüller. The new land across the Atlantic is clearly labeled America. Waldseemüller's map also shows that the world is round.

More detailed maps soon followed as European rulers demanded more information about their new overseas possessions. The Spanish produced maps of the Caribbean and Gulf of Mexico, the English made maps of the Canadian coast, and the Portuguese mapped the coast of Brazil. It was not until the 1520s that people realized that America was one huge continent, with an unbroken Atlantic coastline many thousands of miles long.

This map, dating from the very beginning of the 16th century, exaggerates how close Spain is to America.

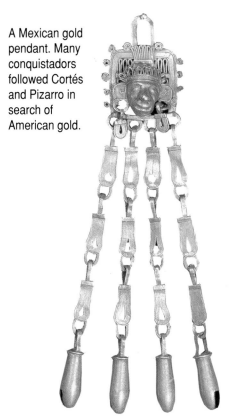

A Mexican gold pendant. Many conquistadors followed Cortés and Pizarro in search of American gold.

An illustration from one of the first books about Mexico, written in the 1540s. The native inhabitants are fleeing from the conquistadors, who are arriving on horseback.

## Two Sets of Indies

In the 15th century, educated Europeans knew that silk, spices, and precious stones all came from a place called the "Indies," by which they meant modern India, China, Japan, and the islands of Southeast Asia. When Columbus sailed west he was determined to find a sea route to the Indies. As it turned out, the land that Columbus discovered was not the Indies. Columbus and the other early explorers gave names to the individual islands, but not to the whole region. However, in the 16th century, after Europeans had explored the Indian and Pacific oceans, the Caribbean Islands became known as the West Indies to distinguish them from the East Indies (the islands to the east of India).

Spanish king. He was a Christian ruler, and if the Native Americans were to be his subjects, they must be Christians too.

At this point, the history of the exploration of America is largely replaced by a story of conquest and forced conversion. All too often, the Spanish Church ordered that natives who would not be converted to Christianity should be killed. With the blessing of the Church and the king, and driven on by dreams of gold and glory, a new type of European arrived – the "conquistador" (the "conqueror"). In a surprisingly short time Spain had acquired a huge American empire. Many conquistadors took part, but two famous names stand out from the rest – Hernando Cortés and Francisco Pizarro.

## The conquest of Mexico

Native Americans living on the eastern coast revealed that Mexico was ruled by the Aztecs from a huge city situated far inland. According to the natives, the Aztecs were very wealthy and their cities were full of gold. In August 1519, Hernando Cortés marched inland with a force of 300 foot soldiers and 15 officers on horseback, according to his own account. Two years later he had conquered the whole of the Aztec Empire.

Cortés was a remarkable soldier, and he was lucky. During his march inland he collected a large number of native warriors who were hostile to the Aztecs, making his army much stronger. When Cortés arrived at the Aztec capital, Tenochtitlán, the emperor, Moctezuma, decided that this pale-faced stranger was an Aztec god, and he surrendered to Cortés. However, the emperor's advisors soon convinced him otherwise, and fighting broke out in which Moctezuma was killed. Although the Spanish conquistadors were outnumbered, the Aztec warriors had been weakened by European diseases. After a few months of warfare, the Aztecs decided that their gods had turned against them, and they submitted to foreign rule. The Spaniards named the conquered territory New Spain.

## The conquest of Peru

Venturing south, the Spanish conquistadors heard of another wealthy empire, that of the Incas in Peru. In 1531, Francisco Pizarro set out to conquer Peru with a force of just 185 soldiers. Once again luck played a large part in his success. The Inca Empire was recovering from a long-running civil war and the exhausted emperor greeted the strangers as friends. Pizarro promptly kidnapped the emperor and held him for ransom. After the Incas had paid a huge amount of gold and silver for his safe return, Pizarro had him murdered. Although the fighting carried on for several more years, by 1533 Peru was firmly under Spanish control. From there, the conquistadors pushed southward into Bolivia and Chile.

In Bolivia, near a village named Potosi, the Spanish explorers discovered a whole mountain made of silver. Through a freak of nature, there was a massive hill that consisted almost entirely of high-grade silver ore. This was wealth beyond even the wildest European dreams.

The swords carried by Cortés and Pizarro during their conquest of Mexico and Peru.

The Potosi "silver mountain," pictured by a European artist in the 17th century (above). Some mining continues today (left), although much of the silver ore has now gone.

## Further explorations

After the conquest of the Aztecs and Incas, there were no more empires to be conquered. However, the conquistadors continued their explorations in search of ever more exotic treasures. One favorite expedition was to find the mythical "fountain of youth" that was supposed to give eternal life to anyone who drank its waters. Other expeditions were undertaken simply to find out more about the New World. By the 1540s the Spanish had explored large areas of what is now the southern United States, and had discovered both the Rocky Mountains and the Grand Canyon.

Some discoveries were made purely by accident. In Peru, in 1541, a Spanish monk became separated from an exploration party. Finding a river, he decided to follow it. Several months later he emerged into the Atlantic Ocean, having traveled more than 2,400 miles down the Amazon River.

## New Foods from the New World

Columbus expected to find exotic fruits on his travels so he was not surprised when the American natives presented him with unfamiliar varieties. As exploration progressed, the Spanish conquistadors came across a whole range of food plants that were completely different from those in Europe. They also realized that many familiar European plants did not grow in America.

Today, when many crops are grown worldwide, it is easy to forget that many commonplace food plants originally came from America, including: corn; cassava (a plant that produces manioc flour and tapioca); potatoes; sweet potatoes; squash; haricot and kidney beans; tomatoes; red and green peppers; pineapples; and sunflower seeds.

Other American plants were less healthy. Columbus was amazed to see the natives sucking rolled-up, burning leaves. However, within 100 years many Europeans had also started smoking tobacco.

## A shortage of labor

Once the conquistadors had looted all the Aztec and Inca treasure, they realized that, although the New World was a source of great riches, these riches could only be obtained through hard work. Precious metals had to be dug out of the ground, and the newly acquired land would only produce crops if it was to become profitable.

A painting from Mexico showing a Spanish conquistador ill-treating Native Americans.

if it was properly tended. The New World, and the West Indies in particular, required a huge labor force if it was to become profitable.

Europeans found the climate too tiring for hard work, often because they insisted on wearing unsuitable European-style clothing. Besides, they had crossed the Atlantic Ocean to become masters, not workers. The problem was made worse by the fact that many of the natives had died. Forced to work in mines and on plantations, their gods overthrown by the new Christian god, they had lost the will to live. The only solution to the problem was to use imported slaves.

## The traffic in misery

Slavery had died out in Europe at the end of the Roman Empire. However, it had continued within the Islamic Empire, which obtained many of its slaves from Africa. Slavery had been reintroduced into Europe some 30 years before Columbus's first voyage, by the Portuguese. While trading down the west

This 16th-century picture of Native Americans "giving" gold to the conquistadors is obviously false. The wealth of America was obtained by forced labor and slavery.

An early 17th-century painting of a slave market in a European settlement in America.

coast of Africa, they discovered that local chieftains would pay for goods with slaves as well as gold.

Faced with a labor shortage in America, the Spanish authorities turned to the obvious source of supply. The first African slaves were taken to the New World in 1510. In 1520, the government issued the first official contract for 4,000 slaves per year to be delivered to New Spain. Within a century, the number of slaves transported across the Atlantic had risen to more than 40,000 every year. Ships from many nations took part in this trade. Conditions aboard ship were terrible: the slaves were packed so closely together that they could hardly move, and they were given little food or water (see picture on page 5). Many became ill during the voyage, and those that died were simply thrown overboard.

Although Columbus was not responsible for what happened after his death, it must be remembered that he himself sent 500 American natives back to Spain as slaves.

## Treasure fleets

American gold was not as plentiful as it had seemed. The native treasuries were the results of centuries of hoarding. However, there were huge amounts of silver ore. The silver metal could be extracted by a newly invented method that used another metal, mercury. By a lucky coincidence, Spain had Europe's only large deposits of mercury. A two-way traffic in metals developed – mercury was sent to America and silver was sent back to Spain.

The silver was usually carried back to Europe, along with some gold and precious gems, aboard specially established treasure fleets. Laden with the wealth of America, some of these treasure

fleets were captured by pirates and the ships of Spain's enemies. Others were sunk because of rough weather. Despite these losses, Spain quickly became the richest country in Europe. Much of this wealth passed on to the rest of Europe through trade, gifts, and bribes to other governments. This gave a tremendous boost to the economic development of Europe.

Ingots and coins recovered from a sunken Spanish treasure ship. Such ships had to survive Atlantic storms and attacks by foreign pirates. A huge fortune still lies scattered on the seabed, and each year divers bring more to the surface.

## Pieces of Eight and Silver Dollars

Some of the silver from the New World was shipped back to Europe in metal bars, but much of it was made into coins before it left Mexico, Bolivia, and Peru. Most of the coins produced were much larger than was usual in Europe, each of them containing eight reals worth of silver (the real was the Spanish unit of currency). These eight-real coins were the famous "pieces of eight" beloved by pirates. The new, large coins were extremely popular in Europe, where they were needed because prices were going up. Other countries also began to produce large silver coins. In Germany they were known as thalers, which becomes "dollars" in English. The word "dollar" was then applied to any large silver coin. So the first American silver dollars were made by the Spanish, about 450 years ago.

A silver eight-real piece, made in South America in 1661. The silver came from the Potosi mines, which in those days were in Peru (as shown on the coin) (see page 27).

The thaler coin was large enough to carry a detailed picture. German thalers often showed a view of the city in which they were produced.

# Native Americans

Corn (above, growing in Peru) was cultivated in America in Columbus's time.

## A rich variety of cultures

At the time of Columbus's arrival, America was populated by a large number of native peoples. Agriculture was widely practiced; corn, cassava, and potatoes were the main crops. In remote regions, a few tribes still lived as primitive hunter-gatherers, existing on wild food and using only stone tools. At the other extreme, many of the American peoples were organized into great empires, and their achievements rivaled those of European civilizations. The Mayans, Toltecs, Aztecs, and Incas all built great empires.

None of the American peoples remained untouched by the arrival of the Europeans. Many had their cultures wiped out. The history of most Native Americans after Columbus is one of oppression. Today, the history of America before Columbus's arrival is especially precious because so much of it has been lost.

## Islanders

When Columbus and his crew first arrived in the New World, they were greeted by a group of happy, smiling natives. Men, women, and children crowded onto the beach, eager to give their strange visitors gifts of brightly colored parrots and bundles of cloth. The natives were naked except for body paint and jewelry, and Columbus noticed that most of them had unusually round faces. Columbus mistakenly called these people "Los Indios" ("the people of India"), and the word Indian has been used for Native Americans ever since.

The people who greeted Columbus were Arawaks. They had migrated from mainland America many hundreds of years before and by Columbus's time they inhabited most of the islands in the West Indies. The roundness of their faces was artificial, produced by binding the soft heads of Arawak babies. Arawak society was ruled by tribal chiefs, but was usually peaceful.

The arrival of the Europeans had a catastrophic effect on the Arawaks. In 1492, there were 300,000 natives living on Hispaniola. Within the next five years about 100,000 Arawaks died of hardship, or were killed.

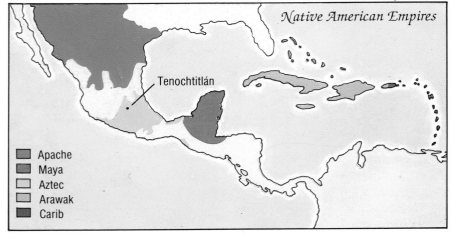

*Native American Empires*

Tenochtitlán

- Apache
- Maya
- Aztec
- Arawak
- Carib

## Local Technology

The Arawaks and Caribs had developed a primitive but successful technology. They lived in villages of thatched huts, and traveled between islands in dugout canoes. The largest canoes, carved with stone tools out of a single tree trunk, could carry up to 40 people.

By comparison, European technology, with its metal tools, gunpowder, and large sailing ships, seemed overwhelming. Nevertheless, some of the Europeans soon realized that they could still learn from the native people. The more observant members of Columbus's crew noticed that the Arawaks slept in woven hanging nets called "hamacas." They borrowed the idea, and soon sailors all over the world were sleeping below deck in hammocks.

European artists of this time tended to show all Native Americans as cannibals, whereas in fact only a few tribes practiced cannibalism.

## Cannibals

The other local inhabitants had migrated to the islands later than the Arawaks. They were the Caribs who lived on some of the smaller islands. From the Caribs comes the name Caribbean Sea, and also the word "cannibal" (a mispronunciation of the Spanish word *caribal*). The Caribs were extremely warlike, and usually ate the flesh of the enemies that they killed in battle because they believed that the strength and courage of the victim would then pass into their bodies. As a result, the Arawaks avoided those islands inhabited by the Caribs. The Europeans followed their example, and the Caribs remained virtually undisturbed for another 200 years.

A Mayan pyramid.

## Mainland civilizations

The greatest of the pre-Columbian civilizations was that of the Maya. Their empire stretched across the Yucatán Peninsula in southern Mexico and into present-day Belize and Guatemala. Mayan civilization developed at different times in different places, but we know that the Mayan people first began building temples and cities around 300 B.C. These temples were remarkably similar to the ziggurats of ancient Babylon, and the pyramids of ancient Egypt. However, archaeologists are certain that there was no transatlantic connection in ancient

A Mayan book showing some of their gods. The gods' names are given in glyph symbols around the edges of each picture.

times and that the similarities are coincidental.

The Mayan Empire was made up of a number of city-states. Each city had a population of about 50,000, with about the same number of people living in the surrounding countryside. The city-states were ruled by kings who were often at war with each other. Captives taken in battle were used as human sacrifices.

The Maya developed America's first writing system, using a series of picture symbols known as glyphs. They were also superb astronomers and mathematicians, producing several very accurate calendars, which were used to chart the festivals of the various gods. Around A.D. 800, the Mayan Empire began to decline, and within 200 years it had virtually collapsed.

# Mexico

The first towns in Mexico were built by the Olmec people around 1000 B.C., and a little later by the Zapotec people. Although the Olmecs and Zapotecs both had highly developed cultures, they were overshadowed by the rise of the Mayan Empire to the east.

Farther west in the Valley of Mexico, a great city grew up, Teotihuacán. In A.D. 500, Teotihuacán was the sixth largest city in the world, with a population of around 200,000.

Around A.D. 900, central Mexico was occupied by invading tribes from the north. The most powerful of these were the Toltecs, who

A massive stone head carved by the Olmec people.

The main avenue of the city of Teotihuacán. The city flourished for more than 400 years, but during the 9th century it was destroyed and abandoned.

established a small empire ruled by priests. Around 1200, the Toltec Empire fell apart into a confusion of warring city-states. New invaders appeared from the north, among them the Aztecs who established the city of Tenochtitlán in 1345. By 1445, the Aztecs had conquered the other city-states and established a strong military empire. At its height, just before the Spanish invasion, the empire contained more than 15 million people.

## The Aztecs

The Aztecs brought little with them that was new. Their buildings used designs that went back to the Maya, and they adopted many of the local gods. They were, however, extremely efficient administrators.

An illustration from an Aztec book. Human sacrifice was an important part of Aztec culture.

Aztec society was ruled by a priest-king, who always came from the royal family. Beneath him, society was organized into a series of privileged groups, such as the nobles, priests, and military officers. Most of the ordinary people were little better than slave workers. The various provinces of the empire had to deliver regular supplies of food, precious metals, textiles, and other items as tribute to their rulers in Tenochtitlán.

The Aztecs believed that their war god, Huitzilopochtli, required daily feeding with human blood. Many people were sacrificed each week, but during special festivals the king would preside over the mass sacrifice of up to 20,000 people at a time. After the conquest, the Spanish founded Mexico City near the Aztec capital. Today, many Aztec buildings lie buried beneath the sprawling modern city. Some of these have been excavated.

## The Feathered Serpent

The Aztecs brought their war god Huitzilopochtli with them, but some of their other gods had been worshipped in Mexico since before the Toltecs arrived. These gods were often associated with powerful animals, such as the jaguar and eagle, but they were usually depicted in human form.

One of these ancient gods was Quetzalcóatl, the feathered serpent, father of the human race and creator of knowledge. Around A.D. 990, the Toltec priests decided that the worship of Quetzalcóatl should be outlawed, and his followers were exiled to the Yucatán Peninsula. Although Quetzalcóatl was officially gone, he was certainly not forgotten. When Cortés arrived, more than 500 years later, the Aztec king, Moctezuma, believed that the pale-skinned Cortés was Quetzalcóatl, returning to save his people.

One of the massive images created by the Nazca people. This one has been called a hummingbird.

## Empires in Peru

Great civilizations had also developed in South America, in the shadow of the Andes Mountains. The early history of these civilizations is not yet fully understood, but Peru appears to have been the main center of activity. Early steps toward civilization were taken by the Chavin people who first built large temples around 800 B.C. Later, two separate empires emerged, the Moche on the north coast of Peru and the Nazca farther south. The people of the Moche Empire constructed a "Pyramid of the Sun" that was over 1,155 feet long. The Nazca left behind them huge pictures, carved into the surface of their land. By around A.D. 500 both empires were in decline. They later became absorbed into the Hari Empire, which extended inland to the mountains.

The people of these early empires constructed cities with temples and other large buildings, and they built large irrigation systems to supply water to their farmland. However, none of the empires was really powerful. This situation changed dramatically with the coming of the Incas.

## The Incas

The Inca tribe moved into the Cuzco valley in Peru around 1300. By the early 1400s, the Incas had formed a small but powerful state. Over the next 100 years, they created an empire that stretched for more than 1,800 miles along the Pacific coast.

The Incas were ruled by a king, the Topa Inca, who had absolute control. Beneath him, society was rigidly organized into a class structure, from civil servants at the top to agricultural workers at the bottom. The empire was administered by a huge number of officials, headed by the Topa Inca's relatives. One of the most remarkable aspects of the Inca state was its network of long, paved roads connecting the Incas' mountain cities. Good roads meant that troops could be sent quickly to crush rebellions, and goods could be transported efficiently. The Incas often used llamas as pack animals, otherwise goods were carried by human porters. Like the Maya and the Aztecs, the Incas had no wheeled vehicles.

# Mountain builders

The Incas' most spectacular achievements were their mountain cities. The most famous of these is Machu Picchu in Peru, which was built on terraces carved from the sides of a steep ridge. The top of the ridge was flattened to make an open site for temples. Although a small city by Inca standards, Machu Picchu covered more than two square miles. When building a fortress, the Incas often used huge stones, fitted close together. Some of the stones have as many as 12 sides, each side carefully shaped to fit its neighbor. At one time people believed that the Incas must have used some secret technology to construct their buildings. However, archaeologists have shown that they needed little more than stone tools.

Llamas in the Andes Mountains in Peru.

The ruins of Machu Picchu, an Inca mountain fortress.

Surprisingly, the Incas managed to administer their huge empire without a written language. Instead of writing, the Incas used quipus – lengths of knotted string. Information was conveyed by the color of the string and the arrangement of the knots (and sometimes small beads). Besides carrying messages, quipus were also used for recording a wide variety of information, from crop harvests to religious calendars.

The Incas standardized their society, and permitted no variation from established Inca beliefs, laws, and customs. This even extended to pottery decoration, and there is little variation between the pottery produced in Ecuador in the north and Chile in the far south. Such uniformity could only be achieved by a very strict government, and naturally this created widespread discontent. The Inca Empire was already weakened by rebellion and civil war when the conquistadors arrived (see page 27).

The ruins of one of the fortified pueblos (villages) that were built about 1,000 years ago. The defensive wall formed a D shape. Inside the wall were 800 rooms, on four and five stories. The round areas were possibly for corn storage. More than 100 such villages were built in Chaco Canyon, in what is now New Mexico.

## Apaches

As the Spaniards pushed northward they met a people who were to remain the bitter enemies of Europeans for the next 350 years – the Apaches. The Apaches were the southernmost of the native inhabitants of North America. Some lived in pueblos, mud-brick villages often built into the sides of canyons (dry river valleys). These Apaches were following an earlier tradition: Between 700 and 1300, other peoples had established a settled culture over much of what is now northern Mexico and southwestern United States. However, most Apaches lived semi-nomadic lives, moving from stronghold to stronghold in an endless round of hunting and making war.

## Cowboys and Indians

The Apaches were superb warriors who knew every corner of their semidesert homeland. However, at first the Europeans had two great advantages – guns and horses. Gunpowder weapons

## Eldorado

Greed for gold continued to inspire many settlers long after the conquistadors had stolen all the riches of the Inca and Aztec empires. One of the most persistent legends among the early settlers, said to be based on native reports, was the existence of Eldorado. Eldorado was usually described as a lost city crammed with gold. However, there were many versions of the legend. According to one report from Colombia, Eldorado was not a place, but a person – El Dorado ("the golden man").

According to this version of the legend, the local tribes would assemble near a lake and cover their king's body with gold dust. The king would dive into the lake, washing off the gold. His followers would then throw golden objects into the lake. Although this lake of gold was never found, it is certainly true that some local peoples used to decorate their bodies with gold dust for ritual celebrations.

were a complete shock to the Native Americans, who long believed that guns were in some way magical. But the Apaches, like some Aztecs and Incas, soon learned that Spaniards could still be killed with stone knives and wooden arrows.

The sight of horses was just as surprising to the Apaches because there were no horses native to America. On the open semidesert, horses were a distinct advantage. However, they were also easy to steal. The Apaches quickly learned how to handle these new animals and became superb riders. Less than 100 years after Columbus's arrival, European "cowboys" were fighting the American "Indians," with both sides mounted on horseback.

A buffalo hide painting showing a horse-stealing raid.

## Horizons

Here are some other places associated with Native American cultures: Monte Albán (a Zapotec city); Lake Texcoco (the Aztec capital was a city of canals); Cuzco and Quito (both Inca capitals); Tula (center of the Toltec state).

# What Happened Later

## Europeanization

The year 1492 marks one of the great turning points in history because the discovery of America was to change the course of European history. Columbus's voyage marks the beginning of what some historians call the "Europeanization of the earth."

## Wealth and power

As wealth flowed in from overseas, Spain and Portugal became incredibly rich. In 1494, a new treaty between the two countries divided America between them, giving Spain nearly all of the New World, while Portugal was confined to the easternmost region of South America. Spain received the larger portion because Portugal had already claimed exclusive rights to Africa.

Between 1490 and 1540, Spain and Portugal established a pattern for success that was later to be followed by other nations. Sea power was used to establish and maintain an overseas empire. Wealth from the empire was brought back to increase prosperity at home, and to increase political influence in Europe.

Although the new empires were the creation of national governments, their success was often due to individual enterprise. Long-distance trade required long-term financing, which was often supplied by commercial bankers. Some of these bankers became extremely powerful. The German banker Jakob Fugger financed the production of Spanish mercury which was used to extract silver ore (see page 30). This meant that, in effect, the Fugger family controlled the output of most American silver mines.

A more extreme case is that of Venezuela. In 1527, the Spanish king leased the whole of Venezuela to another German family, the Welsers. After two decades of exploration, the family decided that Venezuela was not going to make them rich, and this first German overseas colony was abandoned in 1546.

## Spain triumphant

Despite the distraction of America, Spain still had ambitions in Europe. In 1519 the Spanish king, Charles V, was elected emperor of the Holy Roman Empire (present-day Germany). As a result, he became involved in a power-struggle with the rival candidate, the king of France. For more than 30 years France and Spain engaged in a series of wars. Most of the fighting took place in Italy, which was disputed territory. The struggle became more intense when the French king made an alliance with the Islamic Turks who were attacking eastern Europe, but neither side could gain a decisive advantage. Exhausted by warfare, Charles stepped down in 1556. His brother became emperor, the first of the Hapsburg emperors of Austria, and his son became King Philip II of Spain.

King Philip II of Spain.

## Spanish Style

The town of Seville in southern Spain was the port used by the ships engaged in trade with America. As a result, Seville was quickly transformed from a small river port into one of the richest and most glittering cities in Europe. Spanish fashions and customs soon spread among the ruling classes in other European countries, and Philip II was seen as the ideal example of a civilized Christian king.

This fashion for Spanish style also led to the spread of Spanish art and literature. Spain's success had given Spanish writers and painters a new confidence, and artistic achievement flourished. Miguel de Cervantes (1547-1616) wrote *Don Quixote*, a comic masterpiece about a foolish knight. At almost exactly the same time, El Greco (1541-1613) was producing magnificent religious paintings. Other Spanish artists, such as Murillo and Velázquez, also became admired throughout Europe.

The Guadalquivir River in Seville, Spain.

Under Philip, Spain reached new heights of power and glory. The Turks were decisively defeated by a combined fleet of Spanish, Venetian, and other Italian ships at Lepanto in 1571, and Philip was acclaimed as the champion of Europe. His moment of greatest triumph came in 1580, when he made himself king of Portugal as well. The two richest countries in Europe were united under a single, Catholic ruler.

## Rivalry at sea

In 1581, the Protestant towns of the Netherlands rebelled against their Spanish rulers. Spain tried to crush the rebellion by force, but failed. The rebel towns were receiving support from Protestant England. Although Philip had wanted an alliance with England through marriage to Queen Elizabeth I, he now decided to make war instead. In 1588, he sent a huge armada (fleet) to invade England, but it was defeated through a combination of storms and the fighting skills of the English sea captains. Many Spanish ships were sunk, and thousands of soldiers were drowned. Although Spain was to remain powerful for many years to come, the way was now open for other countries to challenge its supremacy. The challenge began when other European nations attempted to establish settlements in America.

## Invisible Killers

Throughout America, small numbers of Europeans achieved overwhelming success against much larger numbers of natives. Superior European technology played a part in these victories. However, the Europeans had another weapon, so secret that not even they were aware of it.

This secret weapon was an array of diseases – ordinary European diseases such as smallpox, measles, mumps, and whooping cough. They had afflicted Europe for centuries, and many Europeans had acquired some immunity to them. However, before Columbus's arrival America was completely free of these diseases, and Native Americans had no such immunity. Within quite a short time, imported diseases were to kill the vast majority of Native Americans. When Cortés marched into Mexico, the country had a population of around 30 million people. A little over a century later, the native population had fallen to about one and a half million, a decrease of around 95 percent.

America later suffered a second wave of new diseases when black slaves brought malaria and yellow fever with them from Africa. These diseases rapidly established themselves in the tropical regions of America.

An Indian suffering from smallpox, in an undated watercolor painting by a Spaniard visiting Peru.

## Patterns of settlement

Within only 100 years of Columbus's death a pattern of European settlement had emerged in the New World. Spain controlled all of South and Central America, except Brazil which was Portuguese. In North America the situation was a little more complicated. In the southwest and Florida the Spanish were in control. Farther north and east, the New World was disputed between the English and the French.

America rapidly became an extension of Europe – a land of opportunity for the ambitious and for fortune hunters; and a place of refuge for others. The first wave of settlers, and probably the most influential, were the Puritans, who left England because of their extreme religious beliefs. The Puritans established themselves in New England and ensured that the ruling classes of North American society became mainly Anglo-Saxon and Protestant. Later, they were joined by people from many other European nations, all of whom made a new home in North America.

By another coincidence of history, many Irish people emigrated to America during the 19th century to escape the

English Puritan settlers making contact with Native Americans.

In 1992, sailing ships from all over the world gathered in New York Harbor to celebrate Columbus's discovery of America. The small ships in the foreground are modern replicas of the ships used by Columbus.

## Horizons
Here are some more cross-connections with the story of Christopher Columbus: the *Mayflower* (the ship in which the Puritan settlers sailed); the Boston Tea Party; Pierre-Dominique Toussaint l'Ouverture (a former slave who became the ruler of Haiti); the Hudson's Bay Company; the Spanish-American War; Geronimo (Apache chief); Martin Luther King, Jr., (an African American leader).

effects of the Irish potato famine. Yet the potato, which had become the staple crop in Ireland, was completely unknown in Europe before Columbus sailed back from America.

## Independence from Europe
On July 4, 1776, the United States of America rebelled against British rule, and eventually declared itself an independent republic with an elected president. In Europe, the ideas of rebellion and republicanism quickly became popular, and led to a long series of revolutions that began with the French Revolution of 1789 and ended with the Russian Revolution of 1917.

In the New World, the creation of the United States began a process of rebellion and independence from Europe. In 1808, at the age of 25, Simón Bolívar began a career of diplomacy and military leadership that freed another large section of America from European control. By the time of Bolívar's death in 1830, Venezuela, Colombia, Peru, Bolivia, and Ecuador had all achieved independence from Spain. In 1821, Mexico also won its independence through armed rebellion.

The United States had several natural advantages over its neighbors. The climate was similar to that of Europe, and the new nation possessed huge areas of good farmland and valuable mineral deposits. The claims of the Native Americans were ignored, and European civilization flourished. By the end of the 19th century, the United States had become an industrial and agricultural giant. During the 20th century the giant turned into a superpower. By 1950, the United States had become the most powerful nation on earth.

# Glossary

**America** By itself, the name refers to North, Central, and South America.

**cannibal** Someone who eats human flesh.

**Caribbean** Relating to or belonging to the Caribbean Sea.

**city-state** An independent state made up of a city and its surrounding district.

**conquistador** (means "conqueror") One of the Spanish soldiers who conquered the Aztec and Inca empires.

**East Indies** An old name for the islands off the south eastern coast of Asia.

**heretic** Any Christian who did not believe in the exact teachings of the Catholic Church.

**humanism** A belief in human values rather than those imposed by religion.

**Islam** A religion founded in the 7th century by the prophet Mohammed. Followers of Islam, who are called Muslims, believe in one god who is called Allah.

**lateen sail** A triangular sail.

**Middle Ages** A term that includes the period in Europe between the 9th and 15th centuries.

**missionary** Someone who travels abroad with the intention of converting other people to a particular religious belief.

**Mongol Empire** An empire established in the 13th century, which included most of the Middle East, Central Asia, and China.

**New World** A European term for North, Central, and South America, as opposed to the Old World of Europe, Africa, and Asia.

**Ottoman Empire** The Turkish Empire founded in the 14th century.

**pre-Columbian** The period of North, Central, and South American history before A.D. 1492.

**Puritans** A group of 17th-century English Protestants who wished to do away with all ceremony in the Church of England.

**Reformation** The establishment of the Protestant Church during the late 15th and early 16th centuries.

**Renaissance** The "rebirth" of European arts and literature during the 15th century.

**republic** A state ruled by an elected leader rather than a hereditary monarch or emperor.

**sultan** A title for the ruler of a Muslim empire or nation.

**trade winds** The steady winds found between the latitudes 30°N and 30°S that blow at a westerly angle toward the Equator.

**West Indies** The islands that lie in and around the Caribbean Sea.

# Further Reading

Baker, Susan. *Explorers of North America,* "Tales of Courage" series. Raintree Steck-Vaughn, 1990

Barden, Renardo. *The Discovery of America: Opposing Viewpoints.* Greenhaven Press, 1989

Burrell, Roy. *Life in the Time of Moctezuma and the Aztecs,* "Life in the Time of ..." series. Raintree Steck-Vaughn, 1993

Conrad, Pam. *Pedro's Journal: A Voyage with Christopher Columbus.* Boyd Mills Press, 1991

Dambrosio, Monica & Barbieri, Roberto. *The Americas in the Colonial Era,* "History of the World" series. Raintree Steck-Vaughn, 1992

Diamond, Arthur. *Smallpox & the American Indian.* Lucent Books, 1991

Dineen, Jacqueline. *The Aztecs.* Macmillan, 1992

Dodge, Steven C. *Christopher Columbus & the First Voyages to the New World.* Chelsea House, 1991

Fradin, Dennis B. *The Niña, the Pinta, & the Santa Maria.* Watts, 1991

Hills, Ken. *The Voyages of Columbus.* Random House, 1991

Hooper-Trout, Lawana. *The Maya.* Chelsea House, 1991

Jacobs, Francine. *The Tainos: The People Who Welcomed Columbus.* Putnam, 1992

Kendall, Sarita. *The Incas.* Macmillan, 1992

Litowinsky, Olga. *High Voyage: The Final Crossing of Christopher Columbus.* Delacorte Press, 1991

Morison, Samuel E. *Christopher Columbus, Mariner.* NAL-Dutton, 1983

Ryan, Peter. *Explorers & Mapmakers.* Dutton Children's Bks., 1990

Soule, Gardner. *Christopher Columbus: Green Sea of Darkness.* Marshall Cavendish Corp., 1991

West, Delno C. & West, Jean M. *Christopher Columbus: The Great Adventure & How We Know About It.* Macmillan, 1991

# Index